Kind Words Uplift

Nourish your Relationships

with

Inspirational Verses

for all

Occasions

BY

CELIA FULLER

Social Media

Connect with me via social media:

 www.facebook.com/pages/
Celia-Fuller-Inspirational-
Speaker-Spiritual-Teacher/
353354161445344

 https://au.linkedin.com/

Scan this QR code with your smartphone to visit my websites:

 www.wholistic-lifestyles.com.au

 www.celia-fuller.com.au

Also by Celia Fuller

The Secret's Out! Men and Sex, Why Women Say No

Pregnancy and Birth, The Conspiracy of Silence

Kind Words Uplift

Nourish your Relationships with Inspirational Verses for all Occasions

by Celia Fuller

Published 2015 by CELIA FULLER

All rights reserved. No part of this publication may be reproduced or transmitted in any form or by any means, electronic or mechanical, including photocopying, recording, or by any information storage and retrieval system, without permission in writing from the publisher. All images are free to use or share, even commercially, according to Google at the time of publication unless otherwise noted. Thank you for respecting the hard work of the author(s) and everyone else involved

Copyright © 2014 CELIA FULLER

Authors and sources cited throughout retain the copyright to their respective materials.

ISBN: 978-0-9941518-1-0

Photography By Canstock , Celia Fuller
Graphic Cover Art :Tasha Wells
Design & Format: Lyn Richards

Dedication

This book is dedicated to life itself and the glorious fullness of the Spirit. Celebrating the journey we all take, coming into a physical life.

Foreword

Celia celebrates the Spirit in all things and believes every interaction we have makes an impact. Through her spiritual journey she has found that everything we do, say or act has an energy of intention behind it and it is up to us, the people of the world, what impact we want to leave as a footprint.

Poetry has been a love of hers since childhood and to this day she continues to write special verses for family and friends as part of her gift giving or writing poems and lyrics requested by others. She is a consummate wordsmith and puts her love and feeling into all her writing.

From the Author

A gentle smile, a listening ear, burst of laughter, celebrating other people's wins all combine to create a powerful ripple effect of loving kindness and positive change. Words whether spoken or written are like an arrow finding its target. You have the power to decide the legacy you wish to gift the world with your own unique imprint. Years of life unfolding are captured in these words. Emotions of care and thought are written here in verse. Take your time to find the one true verse that matches the heart of another. The time you take, with care in your heart, is more powerful than any physical gift, for you are giving of yourself, the greatest gift all humans have.

These verses are my gift.

Celia Fuller

Contents

Social Media ii
Also by Celia Fuller iii
Kind Words Uplift. iv
Dedication. v
Foreword. vi
From the Author vii
Inspirational / New Age / Spiritual 1
Travel 53
Birthday. 65
Birth of a Baby 79
Valentines Day 87
Love 99
Anniversary. 117
Engagement. 125
Proposal. 133
Wedding 143
Friendship. 153
Fathers Day 165
Mothers Day 177
Sympathy For Lost Child 187
In Memory 197
Divorce 207
Thankyou 213
Sorry 221
Difficult Times 229
About the Author 235

Remember the love that surrounds

From the Realms of the Unseen.

Believe anything is possible

And you will evolve beyond the "known".

Let the Wonder enter your heart

And believe

All is One..

Take your time,

Look around,

Search within,

For what must

Be found.

Love, peace and happiness.

Nirvana is here in the very

breath you take

Look to no other do not imitate.

Your life is your own

individual in kind

Honour each second,

sacred is time.

Life is simple easy at best

If you realise Love

is in your every breath.

Dreams Manifesting

Manifest your creation

by matching desires

Set the torch to internal coils.

Let flame and passion burn within

Set your goals to a fiery din.

Be what you want,

you are Creator – Spirit

Expect your goals

come true this minute.

Nature reflects

the

simplicity

of Life

Look within

and

Love

without Questioning

We join together in Love

Love expresses constantly

without judgment

And heals without exception

At the pinnacle

of all human experience

There is Love

Love

is a moment in time

That extends

throughout eternity

The fabric of time

is left with delicate impressions

Of your life passing

with love and expression.

Humans

are an artistic work

in progress

Wisdom

is hidden

in the silence

of the soul.

All the world

there is to see

Nothing compares

to nature's simplicity.

Feel yourself soaring

into the worlds unknown

Open your eyes

and see what's shown.

Nature holds a hidden world

of truth

Wisdom sits expanding new.

Beyond illusions of daily events

Nature sits, weaves and bends.

Power, energy, sweet mystique,

Nature heals and completes.

Connected

Through the heart where

love does dwell

Connections to the Spirit swells.

Individuals connected

through out all time

Back to the Oneness

beyond our minds.

Knock Seek Find

Chance doth have it when

you knock upon the door

Open wide they swing,

answering your primordial call.

Seeking with intent to find,

reveals there is no chance,

For life is but a journey of

synchronistic circumstance.

Peace

Look to the Heavens above

Think of yourself as being a Dove.

Peace can reign in the entire world

Only if you believe You make

Events turn.

Gratefulness

Gratefulness is a reflection

On a life filled with experiences.

It is the opportunity

to see life from

A new and greater reasoning.

Gratefulness comes with the

Maturity of the soul

Forgiveness

Forgiveness occurs after

much reflection

Judgment must be removed

Replaced by acceptance.

To see another's view

is the grandness in growing

Kindness in the heart is all

for the showing.

Forgiveness says

"I love and respect you

For being who you are,

regardless of what you do".

Forgiveness

Remember forgiveness is a powerful tool

Through all of one's life.

Love and be loved with the wholeness

of your being

And good things will come to you.

Wisdom

Wisdom comes from life longing

to understand itself

It is the broadening of perceptions

And the acceptance of others

No matter their ideas and thoughts.

Forgiveness and non-judgment

are essential keys

To unlock the Love

That Wisdom unlocks within Thee

Selflessness

Giving without need

for receiving

Loving without expectation,

Listening without

personal agenda

Caring, for there is

no other way to act.

Acting as though there is

no tomorrow.

Joyous are they who

live in the moment

Each living breath

is a blessing to behold

All praise to the masters who

have walked on earth

And showed the way.

From the heart of God to the mind of man
Love streams forth.
One must open the heart all the more
And do a lot less talk,
For in the silence God does dwell
And in the oceans His joy does swell.
Through nature He shows an Eternal Presence
Of an everlasting stream of patience.

Tread slowly upon the path

And discover wisdom of the heart.

Let your consciousness fly upon

The waves of the ever present OM...

The sound of the Omnipotent within.

Blessed are those who wait

with eternal patience,

Who hold faith within

and are devoted

To trusting all that is shown.

Time heals all sorrows,
Gives perspective and germinates
Wisdom.
The unfolding of ones life
Allows for the nourishment
of forgiveness.
Walk forth in your life knowing that,
Time is on your side.
Let not the past cause anguish
in your heart
But see the beauty of this very day.
Let the morrow cradle a sense
of hope and joy
Within the Spirit of the
Ever Present Being.

Waste not your days on mindless things

But delve into the mysteries

Of life, death and life again.

You are not who you think you are,

For beyond this world is a far greater you

Who experiences the Earth life

as just a dream.

Wake up and know Thyself

And the mysteries of life will be

Given unto you.

The Ever-Present Spirit speaks with a sigh,

Through natures presence and the twilight.

Creatures great and small

Murmur to the Spirit call.

Dawn power evokes secret messages

Through the glimmers beyond Time's veil.

Expansion of the human heart connects to the

Beat of time,

Connected you can be to the

Ever-present Mind.

Sacred is the journey of the heart
Individually it is ours to start.
Judge not the progress of another
Rather look at Thyself and recover.
Wake up from a slumber,
so deep in coma.
Raise your awareness, by looking up
No longer should you duck and cover.
Angels await your questing soul
They are ready to answer
your urgent call.

In the depths a mystery dwells
Behind the hidden is a story to tell.
What you "think" you see,
are thoughts gone wild
What you "Feel" is the truth
of the Inner Child.
Seek not the outer obvious signs
Of amazing gifts that make you smile.
But deeply sink within the oceans swell
Where the core of the spirit does so dwell.
Here in the hidden depths of time
Wisdom born continues to chime.
Behind the heart a Universe Dwells
Love is the truth you know so well
Push not against the tide
of a thinking mind
Dwell only on Love and let it shine.

Awaken

Awaken Child Within
Awaken to the sound of nature rising
Hear the pulse and feel the beat.
Mother Earth is turning up her heat.
Blossom and grow with God's sweet spark
Let the light shine deep in the dark.
Murmuring whispers, nature calls
Expand your mind and feel it all.
So naïve purity dwells
Within the heart where love opens and swells.
The time is right here and now
All you have to do is ask Him How
Celestial Being, Angelic Light
No longer limit yourself, be not in fright
Awaken child within. New days are dawning
And it is your Soul we are calling
To be what you were destined to be
Now is the time
Walk the path and do so faithfully.

Sun rays lighten the early morn

The soul sees it as a new dawn.

Sanctity in the silent air

Spirit breath becomes aware.

Soul awakens to different sight,

Angelic Beings beyond

the broken light.

Man is more than a body,
More than our vagrant thoughts.
Behind the misguided perceptions
Our spirit glows.
Take heart on the journey
Of another human life
Now that within, a flame flickers
Ready to reveal all strife.
To come to know the Spirit
And remember where
you are from,
Takes courage and commitment
That lasts till
the breath has gone.

Love leaves no victims

But gives great opportunities

Of opening oneself up.

It leaves its mark

no matter where it goes,

For love breathes and loves flows.

Did you know that armies stand by,

on your sacred walk,

They whisper words to you

in Angelic foreign talk.

Your heart if it is open,

can hear their loving ways

Your feelings will respond and

encourage you each day.

Judgement, they do not have,

acceptance is their gift

Open your heart

and their direction

You will never miss.

Destiny is Calling

The Spirit's sweet singing is

Heard from afar

Each decision is yours to start.

Step out ever boldly

Let not fear do any holding

Know that Angels watch over you.

See not any failings

Each day is full of changing

Forever bright is the future ahead of you.

Each path is full of growing

Every experience never missed

All is for the learning and a chance

To find Inner Peace.

By the twinkling of the eye

life makes its changes.

Each moment is different

it alters and rearranges.

To live in the now

is your only hope

This way decisions

are easier to cope.

Go with the flow

of life's sweet tune

Experience the mystery

of your Sacred Truth

To breathe is to know God,

To see is to appreciate beauty,

To hear is to understand his whispered words.

To walk is to know the path

To feel is to be connected to all things.

But Love is the greatest of all

It is the Divine expression

Of the God spark within

That reaches out to others

And connects you to the ONE.

Waves pound upon the shore

The conscious mind we do adore.

To move within is a difficult one

The tide urges to look without.

Underneath the oceans swell

A world so different a peaceful spell.

The deep unconscious holds the key

The truth behind life's great mystery

Power sits beyond the soul

Deep within where Spirit dwells.

Stillness sits in everyone

Spirit power joins with the One.

Connected you are

to a greater world

One where love flows and swirls.

Sacred is a human life

Another chance to move from strife.

Untangled by the realms above

Angels work with wings of a dove.

Surrender to the greater force

Awareness waits for so much more.

You are greater than you think you are,

Greater even than the farthest stars.

Connect with the Spirit,

be with the One

Then your life work is surely done.

Flower you are to blossom and bloom.

The Spirit urges "Come home soon."

Your presence is missed

in the higher worlds

But a job is to be done on this fine earth.

Grow, so your seeds can be sown.

Help others to see what you do know.

Give all you can with your sacred life

Each day should be spent by feeling alive.

Treasures you have deep within,

Sow the seeds for your later Kin

Nurture the knowledge, fertilise the soil.

A life so lived is incredibly worthwhile.

Seek with love the golden path

Listen with the mind and the heart.

Feel the truth of the soul's

Urgent search

Seek the truth of Inner Worth.

Take each day as it comes
See the work you have done.
No hard lessons are ever lost,
Growth comes with all the cost.
Accept the way life has been
For your Souls sweet shining
can be seen.

Silver is the clouds sweet lining

Spirit clear, forever shining.

Beyond what your head-mind sees

Wisdom born the Heart-mind gleans.

Between the outbreath

And the Inbreath

Lies the Stillness

Twilight is a moment

Between two worlds

Whilst one is slowly sinking

Another quietly dawns.

Each world is so peculiar

But as precious as a jewel,

Each moment is alive

A sacred path all through.

The nature of the Spirit

Is a sacred ordered thing

Each breath we take connects us

To the sacred worlds within.

To move is to act

To stand is to ponder

To sit is to wait

To breath is to be at One.

Silence, Balance,

The unseeking mind

Stillness surrenders,

The Spirit Shines

Travel

A gift of learning to your hungry heart
The souls sweet singing so willing to start.
Journey forth in the distant lands
Where many teachers await
A pupils eager hand.
This adventure may be filled with youth
But deeper still is the mystery of you,
Great lands will call the Soul's yearning heart
Back in time when karma made its start.
Recognise the pulses of a time yet gone
Know that it is the gift for the soul to finish,
Be done.
Open your heart to the knowledge shown
Unravel the past, one more step to be One.

The world will be a better place

When it sees your smiling face.

Your impact will be noticed

As you travel the distant lands.

Souls will feel you coming

And gather all around.

They'll know they have

Met someone Special

As you travel all around.

HAVE A GREAT TIME

Distant lands are calling

As you plan to leave this morning

Your heart desires more

From this special world.

Answers you may find

As you travel round about.

But never forget the people

Who love you, without a doubt.

We'll Miss You

I wish I was coming with you

To see the sights, you'll see.

I'll be waiting for the postcards

So I can experience

some of it with Thee.

SO ENVIOUS

Adventure is what you are seeking

Beyond this country's door.

I hope it's all what you wish of it,

All of It and More!!

The world does not know what's coming

When you step upon its shores.

They'll feel the earth is trembling

And back away unsure.

Then they'll feel your loving heart

With energy abounding.

They'll come to understand

That your presence is astounding.

CHANGE FOLLOWS YOU

Dreamers caste their thoughts

out in the world,

But you desire action to find

your full worth.

Never one for mediocrity,

travel you insist.

Now you are doing it

You will be sorely missed.

Far horizons beckon you

Adventure is in store.

New people, new places

That you can applaud.

Travel safely my dear friend

And see the things you must.

But never forget back home

The friends you can always trust.

We hold you in our prayers
For every new step taken.
We dream the dream with you
Each day that you awaken.
Safely you should passage
As Angels hear our message,
To hold you with their Love
And bring you back to us.

Angels heard your cry to make a better life,

Where happiness can keep you out of strife.

They nurture every call,

sending out their sacred commands

To bring an army of watchers

over every step you plan.

Go forth to new horizons,

upon the distant shores

Knowing you are safe,

as you respond to your Spirits call.

New Horizons await

upon the distant shores,

New people and places

begging for your applause.

Make sure you leave a mark

wherever you tread,

So you are never forgotten

and you are applauded instead.

Have a Great Time

Life flickers by with such great haste
Young ones think oldies are such a waste.
With age comes reason and love of life
For the older know how to get out of strife.
Housed within, memories so sweet
You are a piece of heaven I get to keep.
You are my sweet heart from ages past
You can't beat that,
I Love you with all my Heart
HAPPY BIRTHDAY

Hold in your heart what is true

Honour the essence of what you know, to be you.

Treasure the years as they gently slip by

Rejoice in life and God most High.

Happy Birthday

Life is but a journey

Of endless ups and downs,

Your life may have uneven grooves

To traverse all around.

Take heart upon your life ahead

Your youthful sparks still blazing.

Watch out everybody

Because you still look amazing!

HAPPY BIRTHDAY

Although speckled hair does grow

And life seems to flash you by

Deep within your Soul that yearns

Is a younger version living inside.

Let not the cynics take your life

Show the younger you're more than wise.

Burst out with courage from the dungeon cave

Where the wilder side has been caged.

Let Loose I Say

Upon The Earth!

Let Them See

What You Are Worth!!

Let each year pass by

With graciousness

And know the soul is

Eternally young

We passed down all we could

We searched within so you understood.

We showed you all that we did know

Now it's up to you to give it a go!

Gifted to us you were
To guide and show the world,
For you to learn.
Beyond all imaginings this you did
You filled my life
And I wouldn't be dead for quids.

For many years

you fought to live

Ruled by your mind alone.

The day has come

to keep out of strife

Your parents no longer

worked to the bone.

Mistakes you make

are yours to be had

Embrace the future,

it's all yours, be glad

It's no longer that of

your Mum and Dads.

Energy plus it's been with you

Bringing you up has been a buzz.

Made us work and clean the loo

Your bedroom is like a wildlife zoo.

Yelled we did over many things

But now you're 18 life will change.

Grow up you must and buy some wings

Soon you'll leave us,

wisdom yours to glean.

HAPPY BIRTHDAY

Come of age, your young mind has.

Journey forth to a new place.

Be sure to know the path ahead

Parents behind look on with dread.

Your heart is yours to direct as your own

It is your destiny that must be grown.

Those behind are your foundation

Use them wisely for future preparation.

Happy Birthday

The keys of your tomorrow

Been given unto you.

A jungle lays ahead for you

to learn and know.

Confident we are in your

mature thoughts

Show us the path that

you have sought.

HAVE A GREAT DAY

Take heed upon the path ahead

Now's the time set sail and spread.

Find the arrow within your heart

Destiny calls urging you to start.

Find the bow that sends you forth

Be caring, kind and of good thoughts.

Have A Great Birthday!

I passed down all I could

I searched within so you understood.

I showed you all that I did know

Now it's up to you to give it a go!

Birth of a Baby

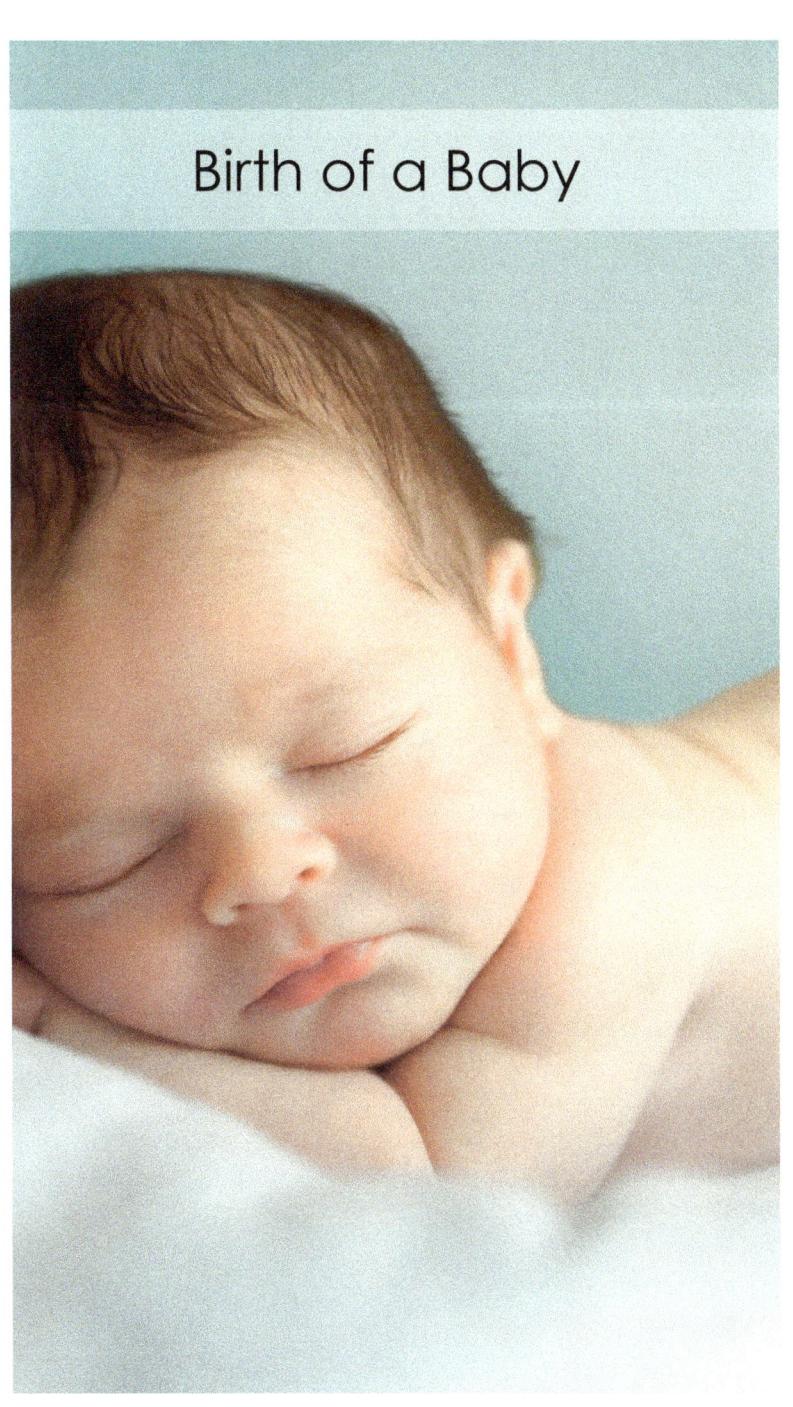

With open arms you welcome

The promise of new life

A wee babe is born

Even as the Angels mourn.

You may not hear the crying

When Angels say good-bye

To the little soul

That left them

And came into your home.

Know that you are a Host

Of a magnificent Angelic Being

Housed within a body,

That we call a Human Being.

Blessed are you who receive this child

Blessed is the child who spends their life

With you.

A child is born on a wave of Love

With Unseen strands coming

from Heaven Above.

The timing has been chosen

by a Greater hand than ours

It is up to you to discover

The Why and the How .

Day by day blossoms bloom.

With life's great Love

a new babe is born.

Precious blessings begins

it's life anew

Completing the bond

between the two of you.

A long time waiting but now its come

All wrapped up in mother's arms.

Precious soul born to you

A great life it'll live, I'm sure it will.

Cry of a new babe can be heard

Parents proud as any devoted birds.

Nestled within your embrace it is

Guided by it's Angel

And sleeps with bliss.

The tide has turned a babe is born
Days will be filled, night and morn.
Hectic will be the early days
It does get better, I think, I pray.
Child will grow from all your love
Guided you'll be by Angels from above.

Rejoice we are,

for your great news

A baby's come to Earth, called school.

Learn it will from

your wisdom true.

Teach it all as knowledge

comes to you.

A gift you've been given

from another world

Yours to cherish,

love and uphold.

Valentines Day

Have you seen me look with wistful eyes?

Have you seen my constant smiles?

Do you know that my heart misses a beat

And my face starts burning

with the heat?

I have admired you from afar

A friendship I have wished

we could start.

I long to hear your words of care

I cannot tell you who I am,

I do not dare.

Your luscious lips fill my mind
I get so dizzy thinking of you
All the time.
I see your smile across the room
I need to know if you like me,
I need to know real soon!
I can promise you my heart is yours
Devoted I've been from night to morn.

Nervous am I of unrequited love
I think of you often
My heart fills with blood.
Is it another that has your attention
Or do I have a chance for your affection?
I dream of the moment you see I exist,
My stomach in knots, I do the twist
I fear my life fading
If you see not, my gazing,
It is you that fills my mind
And makes my life seem worthwhile.

My world has been a tornado

Ever since you came into my life.

My thoughts are whirring madly

The emotions get me into strife.

Daily I yearn to be with you,

To love the whole night through.

Magnetised I am

Do you feel it too?

I walk the beach alone at night

Wondering if you can hear my heart.

I ache to hear your laughter of delight

It fills the darkness with sweet light.

I whisper of my love for you

To the twinkling stars.

I pray to God that you will soon know

The secrets of my heart.

Crystal clear I feel my love

Powerfully urgent, comes from above.

Guided I was to find you here

To find and love you very dear

Powers within pulled me through

To tell you how much I love you.

Office love is a forbidden fruit
I look at you and do loop the loop.
Picture perfect you numb my mind
Loving caresses imagined all the time.
Work I cannot even try to do
Thoughts of you are all that get me through.
I wonder often if you feel the same
If I don't find out soon
I feel I'd go insane.

The cutest bum I ever saw

In those shorts you turn me raw.

Trembling knees on mine it makes

I wish it was me who was your date.

You are so hot with that cute little bot.

Kissing your lips are my sweet dream

If you tell me that you like me

I know I would scream!

My eyes are riveted to

your gorgeous face

My heart skips a beat,

it's never done that.

Your gentle lips

I wish to taste

I've fallen for you and that's

a fact!

Sweet Love fills the air,

I look in your eyes without a care.

A captured moment

my heart misses a beat

I feel my body fill with heat.

A feeling of passion it may be true

Yet the truth be told

It's from my deepest love for you.

Love

As I sit next to you

I yearn for you all the more.

I realise it is you

I truly adore.

Even as the years pass by

I feel that precious link

Which brought our hearts together

And will never be extinct.

Loving you has been easy

Your gentleness complete,

I am forever thankful

That we were allowed to meet

Delicate are you

You are too good to be true

Past Love Future Life

The twinkle in the eye I see

Wondering what you mean to me.

With a surety I cannot surpass

I know I've known you in the past.

Echoes of a lifetime with Joy and Love

You came to me in visions, so vast.

Exquisite versions of lives entwined

It is you who is always on my mind

In the twilight of the night

Your whispered words were heard.

For out came a meeting

Where mutual love did burn

And the precious Gift of love you gave,

Finally Returned.

Sweetness is in the flair of a loving hand

Rare is you who Loves regardless of demands.

You teach me all about loving

In a special kind of way

Those gentle eyes and caring touch

Send all my cares away.

You treat me like a precious jewel

That washed upon your shore.

In my heart you found a place

And now it is you I adore.

I am not a Man of many words
Whilst earthly pursuits fill my time.
Practical is my nature in all I approach
But now thoughts of you fill my mind.
So when it comes time in life
To express how I might feel,
I find there is inadequacy
That I try not to reveal.
I hear the words of poets
and wish I could speak like that to you,
Yet one would think that only composers
Had such a gift with verse.
What I am really trying to say
In a roundabout kind of way
Is, I treasure the ground you walk on
My love grows for you each day.
I know not what I'd do
If I couldn't spend my life with you
You fill me to completion
I hope you feel it too.

Roses are red violets are blue

For all our days I've

never stopped loving you.

Leaves are green, the Earth is brown

I love you even when you frown.

Vodka is clear, beer is amber

I bet you think I'm a bit of a charmer.

Mangos are orange, bananas cream

You are the girl of my night-time dreams.

Winds rustle with speechless words

Doves fly in a peaceful world.

Butterflies flap in a blissful haze

My senses have awakened

As I sink into your gaze.

A longing has been answered

When you entered my life.

Love ricochets through me

When I see your smile.

There is nothing I think is greater

Than finding the love of your life

And dream of a future

With you standing by my side.

Interwoven

Two lives entwined in a lover's knot
Where we came from I have not forgot.
A friend at first you have been
Now it's love I do see,
Perhaps in another time
we journeyed forth
Feeling love and each others worth.
Linked way back in past distance life
Together again to work out the WHY.
Love seems to pursue a mysterious track
Karmic records send us back
Alone I feel not, when you are near
Completion, Onenes, I love you dear.

My wife of many years

You are so important to me

Aging may have crept in

But to me you're still the

Sweetest thing.

Your heart is truthful

Our friendship fruitful,

For throughout all this time

You are still the girl that

Fills my mind.

My body is weary, the aches come and go.

You hear me daily having a moan.

I see the eyes rise to the ceiling

Just remember my heart still has feelings.

I may seem decrepit in body strength

I may not even be able to help move the bench.

But I can still tell you my love is strong

And within my soul I still sing the lovers song.

I'm grateful for your patient ways

Never enough words to sing your praise.

Never forget how much I love you,

My heart still aches when I look at you.

Cranky man, are you

Stranger am I for loving you.

Loved and lost,

I have so many times.

Terrified I am to admit

what's on my mind.

I cannot yet say "I Love You"

but I fear

Its getting closer each day

I spend with you.

Be careful of my heart

For it's so easy to hurt

Take your time to see

What I am really worth.

I love hard but say it little

To say it often just makes it

Sound like piffle.

I know you need the words

To ease an aching heart

Maybe this card could be

Considered my little start.

Feelings for you I try to hide

I try to push back the rising tide.

Love overtakes at every turn

It is for you that I always yearn.

Thoughts of you rupture my sleep

Cascading sensations wake the deep.

Love is ripe and always true

My life completed when I met you.

Time they say is on your side

My feelings for you I cannot hide.

Time to me is the enemy

I fear that time may lose you completely.

I struggle to get my feelings out

It's not because of any doubt.

I am a man of quieter ways

To speak of deeper feelings

Haunts me for days.

I see others who give all the attention

I panic with thoughts of not getting a mention.

Forgive me for my lack of romanticism

I know you've been waiting for my decision.

The Answer is "Yes, I love you

With all my heart and mind

I pray that time will be on our side."

To me, you are like the ocean,

Endless seas and new horizons.

Each day has been an adventure

Frontiers broken and then entered.

You astound me with your drive,

A heart that won't back down.

My life with you has been so immense,

As vast as the oceans swell.

HAPPY ANNIVERSARY

You have no idea the gift you are to me

You do your best to try and please.

You shift your life to fit into mine

For that I think you are divine.

I try to assist you all I can

But I see you're stronger than any man.

My life takes on a different hue

When I spend precious moments

looking at you.

Love has come and carried us away

...years later I still adore you to this day.

It's been an interesting path

Spending my life with you.

... years of marriage

has been quite hard.

But through all the knocks

Love has not been blocked

And I still find myself

devoted to you.

Grown has my soul become,

Spending a life with you.

You've made me see things differently

Inspired with lots to do.

My world opened up the day

I married you.

Happy Anniversary

My life would be so different,

If you had not come round.

A part of me would be lost

And maybe never found.

You helped me find my destined path

Thankfulness lives daily within my heart.

I could never have imagined

The life we've come to live

It's been really quite eventful

Memories I'm glad I never missed.

This time with you has been surely great
You've lived this life as my great mate.
I've loved you through the ups and downs
You always were the sweetest girl in town.

Years have passed since we first met
I saw your eyes and felt so blessed.
Our marriage has been a great source of pride
Today my love for you, I cannot hide.
Each day I've spent with you
Has been ever unfolding and brand new
Loyalty has blessed us all along.
My love,
You are where my heart belongs.

Engagement

Engagement is your chance in life

To ponder on your choice,

Time for dreaming

And speaking with one voice

Commitment to be together

Has its ups and downs.

But the love I see in your eyes

Shows you are ready for this

Right Now!

So Happy For You Both

Blessed you have been

To find your loving match.

HAPPY ENGAGEMENT

Hand in hand you walk together,

down the golden path.

I see it in your eyes the love within your heart

Make this be a precious time

of heart felt memories.

For marriage is the time to fulfil

All those longed for dreams.

CONGRATULATIONS

Celebration is at hand

I heard the wonderful news.

I shook my head in wonder

Hoping it was true.

Now you have confirmed it

I am over the moon.

FANTASTIC NEWS!

A ring upon the finger, gentle words proposed

Love has moved great mountains

Where you go from here no body knows.

The mystery has begun, a journey of the senses

A life together now commences

Behold the wonder in this life

When two people choose to be,

Husband and Wife.

Dizzily you soar, two souls in love.

Angels sitting watchfully,

From the realms of the above.

Entwined are you in the lover's embrace

Congratulations on your sweet fate

Love has found its mark
Between the two of you.
Sacred is the tryst
Within the space you now move.
Promises of marriage are
Like a silver sword,
One your souls been yearning
With love the sacred call.
Your match was made in heaven
Before you even met,
The sword of your two spirits
Made sure you did not forget.
Now you found each other
The dance begins again.
Remembering always that lovers
Should always be friends.

Proposal

Winds rustle with speechless words

Doves fly in a peaceful world

Butterflies flap in a blissful haze

My senses have awakened

As I sink into your gaze

A longing has been answered

When you entered my life

Love ricochets through me

When I see your smile

There is nothing I think is greater

Than finding the Love of your life

And dream of a future

With you as my wife

WILL YOU MARRY ME

Love is a moment in time

That extends

throughout eternity.

Constant is the energy

that makes

our two hearts beat.

Love synchronises

our precious lives

I yearn for your life

to join with mine

Will You Marry Me?

Birds fly with courting song

In my life you belong

I see the birds build their nests

I think with you, I could be the best.

They sing and dance to a different beat

But they still understand the precious heat

Serious courting and eggs they lay

I hope you will join me in the same way.

I long to be with you for the rest of my life

WILL YOU MARRY ME?

Tonight I see you are looking divine

I'm sure it's not because

I've been drinking too much wine.

Each morning when I awake

And see your gentle face sleeping,

I notice deep within,

An ache of my heart weeping.

I realised then my life is not my own

I knew I wanted us to buy a home.

To have a bundle of kids

And lots of friends to mix.

I would not survive

if you chose a different life

That is why I am asking

"Will you be my Wife?"

*I'm normally a courageous man
Who speaks my mind and loves the action.
I do not usually use the cowardice of the pen
But tonight I seem lost for words as
I struggle for your attention.
The days have been long,
My thoughts filled with you,
Your beauty simply dazzles me
Catching words within my throat.
By now I should be on my knees
To ask if you would Marry me.
Instead I chose a poem
To make the words come out straight.
So here it is my sweet, sweet love.
"Do you think I am worthy,
To walk a path with you?
Would you possibly consider
Marrying me?"
Because I dearly would love you to.*

Beauty you are in every breath you take

A proposal it is, that I would like to make.

I ask this question seriously

Acknowledging our ups and downs.

"Will You Marry Me

And walk a new path with me now? "

When I see you, my heart does weep.

Joy I feel when you are near

I realise I love you so very dear.

Marry Me, my love of loves.

I pray you will say yes

I pray to God above.

I know you say you love me
But I am not always sure.
I fear one day you will just get up
And walk out my door.
I know my feelings are hard to read
And eloquent words I cannot say.
But the love I feel for you
Just gets stronger by the day.
I mumble and I fuddle
And frustrate you to bits
But Love, I was wondering
If you and me could get hitched.
You know what I mean
Well I hope you do,
If you say you'll Marry me
I'd just about fly right over the moon!
"My Love
Will You Marry Me?"

Beauty you are in every breath
A kind heart and delicate face.
My soul lights up to dazzling depths
When I hold you in my arms
The answers to life's questions seem so clear
When I am with the one I Love so dear.
Time standstill when I look in your eyes
I see the universe and the twinkling stars.
I cannot remember a time when peace
Was so easily had.
If you chose not me, I think I'd go quite mad.
You give me reason to take each step
And breath another day.
Life without you I could not reason
My love for you shows the way,
My aching heart cannot go on
The pressure builds and weighs a tonne.
A question torments me to this very day
Now is the time without delay.
WILL YOU MARRY ME?

Wedding

Two hearts have felt the visions of Love

Converted from the glory of Heaven above.

Yet each really knows Heaven lays within

Look deeply into each other, let your hearts spin

Acknowledge the God within each you adore

Hold each other close forever more.

Never forget the force that entwines

as you begin life as

Husband And Wife

Sacred is your marriage joining

Beautiful is your love outpouring.

This day is full of great intentions

Forever togetherness, we hear you mention

Be not this day just for fairytale endings

But a life where two friends are

constantly blending.

HAVE A GREAT LIFE TOGETHER

You came together on this day of days

We look at you both and sing your praise.

When the lights go down, all people gone,

Your life together is where you belong.

Whilst your love is bright

and pure of intent

Make sure you live it

as though heaven sent.

For in the times when lust is gone

It's the friendship that will help you

keep going on.

Congratualtions

On Your Marriage

A lover you chose till the end of days

A companion who will support

and give praise.

Kindness can be gifted to each other

Accept that some things are

not good for the other.

Communicate well, Be not closed off.

If mistakes are made, try not to mock.

Hurt not so easily or take defence

This is your lover that you felt so intense.

It's easy to forget the joyous love and vows

Give each day a special place

And just live in the Now

Step by step you face each other

Saying the words "I Do"

Precious moment halts all time

Before the spell is woven.

This day of days is sacred

Opening up a whole new world,

Where changing is expected

Just like the moving

Tide.

Congratualations

On Your Marriage

Together you stand in front of us

With devoted love.

Choirs of heavenly visitors

Watch from realms above.

Sacred is your contract

To live a life anew.

Added to the memories

Is our love for both of you.

Gentle is the hand of love

That bind the two of you.

Holy is the space you make,

With your chosen words.

Blessed are you to discover

Each others special worth.

Have A Lovely Life Together

CONGRATULATIONS

ON YOUR MARRIAGE

Marriage is

Two seeds planted

In fertile soil

GROW WELL IN YOUR LOVE

AND LIFE TOGETHER

In the twilight of the night

your whispered words were heard

For out came a meeting

where mutual love did burn

And the precious Gift of love you gave

Finally Returned

Congratulations on Your Wedding

Friendship

Flowers bloom all over this world

Within my heart friendship for you does dwell.

Mates accept the good and the bad

When I stuff up you don't even get mad

I thank you for your thoughts

and insights too

I miss the good times when

I'd do/go......................with you

THANKYOU FOR BEING

A GREAT FRIEND

We stand alone on earth's fine crust,

In God it is our hearts must trust.

Friendships sometimes come and go

Lovers cease, children grow.

We are on a journey from Spirit, man to Spirit.

It is in the aloneness that man finds the ticket,

Pathways back to the eternal light are varied,

Each unique being may dance and parry.

Our home back to oneness is through the heart

How we get there is yours to start.

I Cherish

Our Friendship

Winds of time blow between us
Past is gone, the future is near.
You are the key-holder to
my precious past.
With you I walk deep in my heart.
A key-holder is a guardian to
life records long gone.
Yet the past echoes in the soul
Telling the future where
I have come from.

THANKYOU FOR
HAVING BEEN
A PART OF MY LIFE

In life many hardships

go and come.

It's so much easier when

good friends support

And help you to overcome.

The precious link of friendship
Grows stronger by the day.
You help me see things clearly
No matter, Come what may.
Life is so much easier
When you know a friend is there.
The times we've had together
Joyful beyond compare.

I feel your caring heart even when apart

No matter what the story,

you always lend your ear.

You listen very quietly and

give me strength each day.

Your friendship is inspiring I pray it always

Remains that way.

Did I ever thankyou

for all the support you give?

Did I ever tell you

that you make me feel so big?

My confidence seems to grow when you

Listen with your heart.

I thank the Lord always that our friendship

Found a way to start.

Strength is found with

your caring words

Your friendship is

A Million Dollars Worth.

I miss your presence daily
Now that you have gone away.
I hope you hear my special words
And remember them each day.
I treasure all the stories and
The laughs we often had.
Even when the tears did flow
You always made me glad.
Though it often saddens me
That you are not here.
Memories of your friendship
I hold onto very dear.

Life is like a rich tapestry

Full of weaves and bends.

Interwoven with the journey

Stories often mend.

Each new strand is special

Stands out in the crowd.

They define the picture of what

Your life is really about.

Each strand resembles friendship

Of strength just sitting there.

Within each waking moment

The most important is

those who care.

When all others are gone,

you remained by my side

The goings tough, you did not hide

Blessed is your friendship,

In my Heart you reside.

Fathers Day

Fathering is a precious gift

With it comes many a hitch.

Open your heart to a child's world

You'll hear their hearts if they are hurt.

Hold them close to ease their pain

With your help they can be happy again.

Know you have the power to make or break

Love then deeply, but not in haste.

Dad

The strength is mine to be had
You taught me to think clearly
which I am glad.
There never was a time
I did not look up to you
Sometimes I missed you,
which made me blue.
You are the foundation
of my adult life
Your words often guided,
"To keep me out of strife."
I did my best with the life you gave.
Daily your guidance helps me add
To what I have made.

DAD

Forceful strong and removed are you

Sometimes I wondered how to impress

or what to do

I kept looking for your outward love

And found it hard to see

Later I realised it was the work ethic

you gave to me

I saw your love through the work you did

I now understand.

You loved me by what you could give.

I Am So Grateful

For Your Love

A soul seeks the parents it needs,

To grow with love and wisdom to heed.

I see now how I chose so well

My love and gratefulness

In my heart does swell.

Dad you made it!

You saw it through!

I'm all grown up

because of you.

You kept me safe,

clothed and fed.

Because of that

I've got a great life up ahead

Happy Father's Day

To be a father

has its moments.

I hope I was not

too much of a torment!

Take heed a father is in need of loving

Beyond the authoritarian wall,

Is a man in need of hugging.

So don't stand back

Teach him how to love

Grab him with a Big Bear Hug!

You are my rock and gentle ear

You are my foundation

When I need to shed some tears.

You've loved me like no others

Because you are my dear, dear Father.

You advised me to be strong

And to know what is wrong

And told me to watch out for all the boys.

For that I am so grateful

And my heart is always hopeful

That I'll find a man

comparable to you.

Sadly you missed most of my life

The growing up and all the strife.

I worried that your love was gone

Now I know I was so wrong.

I cherish the scattered pieces

Of my sweet memories,

Of you visiting me

in my childhood dreams.

Although I still hold some pain

I know your love is strong

In my heart love dwells.

In the part where you belong.

Stranger you are to me

Blood is thicker than wine

I remember precious moments

When you were my father divine

I long to know you better

And understand myself

For you have the power to

Unlock my inner worth.

I long to know what's on your mind

And discover who I am.

Father you are a part of me

A part I want to call friend.

PLEASE MAKE CONTACT

As a child I saw your

hardened knuckles

And wondered how they came.

Today I have the answer

for mine are now the same.

You taught me how to protect

and keep the family safe

Each day I do the same as you dad

I don't even hesitate.

My skills and manhood blossomed

because of your care

My respect for you unbounded,

I hope you are aware.

Mothers Day

MUM

Mum you taught me to Love

And give of my heart

You showed how to give life

A positive great start!

Cherished are you to me

You gave me life and honoured me.

Your time was not all yours

But love you gave to a baby on all fours.

That baby grew up with your gentle heart

My life is great because you gave it a start!

Happy Mothers Day

The cherished moments you did give
Gave my life one big lift.
You loved with intensity
And disciplined with difficulty,
I did not see it at the time
How parenting can sometimes
ravage the mind.
You continued with greatness
And saw it through,
For That I have blessings just for you.
You taught me how to handle life
Even when you wanted peace and quiet.
Your Gift to me was the willingness to share
When compromising your freedom
Was difficult to bare.
I now know your life was not so easy
But I need you to know
I love you completely.
Without your nurturing,
guidance and wisdom
My life could have been infused
with negative reason.
Instead I see my life in a positive light,
And for that I thankyou with all my might
HAVE A LOVELY MOTHER'S DAY

Mum you did what you had to

Even when I made you feel blue.

You scolded as was needed

And held me when I pleaded.

Your loving touch seemed to fix all the wrongs

Your gentle words taught me to be strong.

Today I speak as a man

I look back at my life feeling glad.

You have been my greatest asset

You put my spirit to the test.

I now see the world through maturer eyes

And the love I feel for you

Sometimes makes me cry.

Mum You Are The Greatest

MUM

You rose beyond the shadows

From the darkness of the night,

Every low point ever felt

It was you who fixed my life.

Your easy ear and wise words

Kept the path so straight.

But on the odd occasion

Despair would run me late.

You loved me through my childhood

And in the terrible teens.

You always lifted when I fell

and cared when I was in need.

THANKYOU FOR LOVING ME

I thankyou for all you work

And loving through it all.

Mum you're really special

And I'll love you forever more.

You who gave birth to me
Is as precious as the stars.
You gave up your life
As mine began to start.
Your desires were put on hold
So I might have your love.
You cherished me so fondly
I thankyou from my whole heart.
THANKS   MUM

Love is precious, love is kind.

Mum you are always on my mind.

I wonder how it was for you

all those years ago,

Did you really like it

Or did you call us "SO and SO's"

Either way it does not matter

Respect for you has grown.

I see and hear your voice

Coming out my very own.

I long to be near you

And compare the terrible twos.

I miss your gentle knowledge

And wish to know how it was for you.

I Miss You

What skill a mother has

to keep the home afloat,

Forever calming nerves

that usually rock the boat.

You kept an even temper

and spread your loving care

Mum I love you much,

I hope you are aware.

Friendship and guidance

I hold with deep cherishing

You as my mum is

the greatest life Blessing

Sympathy For Lost Child

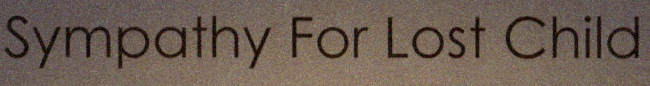

See your dearest child

Taking steps in the world above.

Feel the Angels singing

As they wrap them with their love

Heaven had some greater plans

That only yours could fill.

The beckoning call came earlier

Whilst the innocence was stilled,

For that's how Angels like them

For the work they have to do.

Be happy that they came

As a gift in your hands,

Hug them one last time

Then release them to

The Divine Plan.

So much love wrapped in one.

Sorry for the loss of your Son

Cut was his life, a little short

God knows His greater worth.

Land beyond he now walks,

Loved by Angels with whom he talks

WE ARE HERE FOR YOU

The loss of your baby we are sad to hear

Great hopes you had to love it dear

Reasons are not easy to gather or find

The reality of its life

Will be forever on your mind.

Others may say "Just try again"

A child you lost you can't pretend.

Shortness of life it may have been

Your heart knows the soul who chose to begin.

Sad we are to know the painful cost

Of the life you loved and now have lost.

We Are Here For You

Precious baby came to you,

From a world within the clouds.

Special times were had by you

Before she went back home.

Blessed baby, times were short.

Memories ever-sweet for you to talk.

A child is never replaced

And leaving not understood.

Why they came and leave again,

We hope is for the good.

We question God's bigger plan

For taking your child friend.

Angels know the answer

And love to you they send.

Tragedy is sad to hear
In anybody's life.
When we heard of your distress
We asked the question " Why"
No reasons were apparent
And know not, what to say.
Only that we are here for you
Even when others have gone away.

A pearl of wisdom came to you
And left it's golden spark..
Sweet child of yours has gone away
But left its loving mark.

Broken hearts take time to mend,

Love links the soul and will never end,

No matter the length of time you spent

God's love had another intent.

A child remembered,
our baby you mourn
Crestfallen, a life shredded forlorn
Behind you I stand to catch your fall
Picking up pieces from off the floor.
When you are weary
and cannot face the world
I stand like a barricade
in my own tearful blur
I may not speak of the pain
within my heart
For I am the man who
should have no tears start.
Yet know that I am here suffering
lost dreams with you
Together we stand praying,
one day hope renews.

I am Here My Love,
Silent but beside you

In Memory

Spirit Lives On

Breath of wind in the air

A sparkle in the stars

The cleansing feel of rainfall

The replenishing warmth of the sun

The comforting glow of the Moon

A restless roar of the Ocean

chuckling and chortling of a stream

A gentle smile flickers across your face

A warm glow enters your Heart

… is that you?

The Spirit lives on in those left behind.
Love lingers as a melody on the wind
As the freed Soul soars to the Unknown.
Angelic beings welcome with open arms
With Holy Love they cherish and care,
Allowing their new charge
to become fully aware.
Glory be to the soul who's found
A greater freedom than the earthly bound.
To them life has begun anew
Take heart, for they now send
Their love to you.

She sits amongst the clouds alive
Whispering words of love to you
Although she feels your
desperate pain
She knows her life was
not in vain.
Her thoughts reach out
in the night-time hours
Hoping you can feel her
in the now.
Enveloping you in her life anew
She is delighted to be watching
From a Room With a View.

The sadness you feel right now will pass

When many full moons have long gone.

Let the memory of your beloved mother

exist beyond all time,

In the sacred heart of the Soul

It is here, where the joy still is

For her ever having lived at all.

Mother's life a precious gift

Devoted to her child's every stress.

She is the strength

behind every thing in life

She is the woman

who became your father's wife

Cherished be, her great memory

We send our prayers to your family.

Laughter rings out loud

From Heavens open door

His journey is nigh but over

It is his life we now applaud.

May your grief be turned to joy,

May your pain be turned to hope.

May you who feels such sorrow

Find the strength to face tomorrow.

Dimension open, time stands still
He steps across the line that separates
Him from you.
He feels your love extending with every
New found step
And knows you've always loved him
One second to the next.
Surrounded by heavenly hosts
That take him by the hand
He realises he is not gone from you
He's just traveling in another land.
So when it's all said and done
Relief washes over his crinkled brow
He smiles a great big smile at you
and says
" ....
I love you"

Let not sorrow fill your mind

The pain will lessen given some time.

Now is for reflection

and love well tendered

Celebration and Joy, a life well

Remembered.

Divorce

My heart lets you go to a greater life
I hope you find happiness without the strife.
As individuals we began our path,
Joined we were for a hopeful start.
Untangled now, we become individuals again
Unweaving the promises and vows
To stay together until death does end.
I Set You Free
To Find A Greater Peace.

Joined together we were by hopes and dreams

Sadly those hopes are dashed, or so it seems.

I'm sorry for the despair and remorse

Now that I set the sails for my own course.

Uncharted territory it surely is

But I leave to seek some kind of peace.

Unwoven from you I wish to be

I release the power that bound you to me.

Vows have been spoken

With love my heart was given

Sadly it's time I released you from me.

Power of our spoken vows

Committed us to giving love a whirl.

We strode through life with

hope in our hearts

Sad it is now that we

have decided to part.

Time has come to let each other go

Releasing the ties that bind me to you.

Go forth with new freedom

May peace find its way into your heart.

Untangled I wish to be.

Freedom I need, to go as I please.

Hold me not back

I've set my sails, I cannot tack.

My course is made, my mind is set,

The shores of love I have left.

With the words that bound us together

I release the energy that has tethered.

Power I give back to you

I take my own for a new life to pursue.

No amount of words on paper
Can summon up my heart
Gratitude is greatest,
The list too long to start.
Your kindness is not forgotten
It is lodged within my mind.
To show my deepest appreciation
I'll pass it on in kind.

Speechless I am to your care and concern

If not for you I would feel quite alone.

Thank you for your kindness that's full of grace

Each time I see you, it lights up my face.

Wonderful soul I was blessed with

Who saw my needs

and proceeded to give.

The gift of your heart

and splendid energy

The task made easier

by your splendid company

Your help has been

immeasurable,

Your devotion complete.

Thank you, for being near

In our moments of

greatest need.

Your support has been marvelous

And heart felt through and through

You've made everything easier.

That requires a special hug for you!

Thank you for your warm kind gifts

And seeing us get married.

Your witness of this special day

Creates memories

Within our hearts we carry.

The time you took to care

Has meant so much to me

A portion of your life gifted

From a heart of generosity.

With Great Appreciation

I'm sorry for the words I said

I did not say them with hurtful intent.

Anger brings out the worst in me

The hurt I caused you brings me to me knees.

Believe me when I say my sorrowful words.

To not be your friend is just absurd.

Too many words have been said

I wish my anger could be gone instead.

I know I hurt you deep inside

It is my head I wish to hide.

I'm sorry for the hurt

And all the angry words

Please believe me when I say

I want our friendship to work.

With great regret I saw your hurt,

Words we said got out of sorts.

Upon reflection

I know you were right

I'm sorry that I got so uptight.

Friendships are a precious gift
Full of acceptance and sharing
Reaching out and
Showing each other the caring.
I wish I could take back
the words I said,
My heart feels sorry and
I feel quite dead.
Please forgive me
for what I have done.
I wish I could undo
all that is wrong.

Forgive me for my recklessness

My raging ways and thoughtlessness.

I'm sorry that I missed your special day

I knew it was important

And there is no excuse to say.

I miss the special times we spent

Inside your caring home.

I'm sorry that I blew it

And the good times are gone.

A special friend you have been,

One that is not often seen.

So regretful am I

That you are no longer

A friend of mine.

I'M SO SORRY

Difficult Times

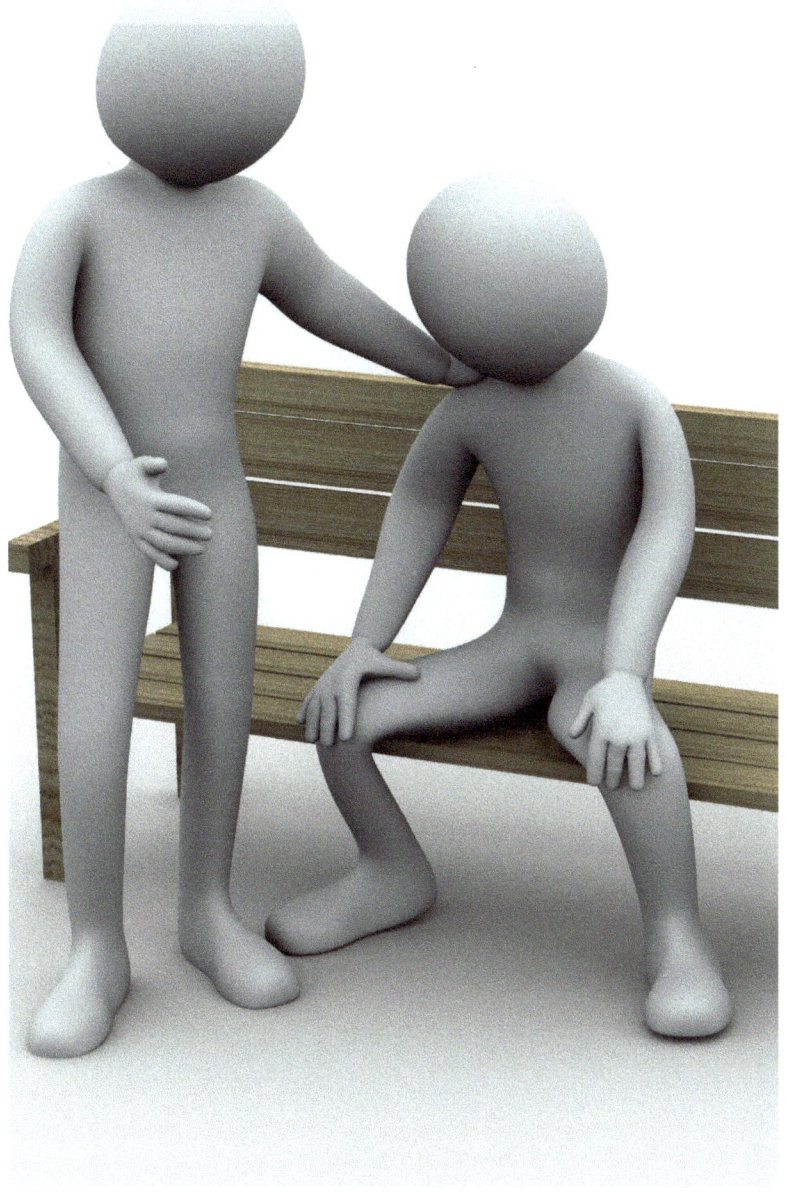

Together you stand in life

As all families must

Look to each other

As those you wish to trust.

Even when the going gets tough

You should always stand hand in hand.

For it is the journey of the family

To truly understand,

That through the faults

or jagged decisions

True Love shines through

And makes no demands.

BE GENTLE WITH EACH OTHER

Life is tough in so many ways
We stand by you, this very day
Friends can ease the pain and hurt
Help you think and ease the work.
We are here through these worrying times
Allow us to support you from behind.

Can We Help?

Life is tough in so many ways
I stand by you, this very day
Friends can ease the pain and hurt
Help you think and ease the work.
I am here through these worrying times
Allow me to support you from behind.
CAN I HELP?

Go forth with trust and faith in God

Know that your prayers

are being heard.

Even when they don't seem answered

Angels come and do the work.

Peace of mind,

clear honest thoughts

Will be the answer

you earnestly sought.

STAY FOCUSSED.

Beyond the turmoil there is a path
Once more leading beyond the Dark.
Each day with a sigh, a deeper breath taken
Resurrecting your strength removing
hesitation.
Let faith lead you towards the
step of tomorrow,
Begin a new morn where laughter can
follow.

About the Author

Celia Fuller is a well sought after Australian Inspirational Speaker focusing on the celebration and upliftment of the human spirit in all aspects of life. She draws upon over 20 years of experience as a Spiritual Teacher, Wholistic Lifestyle Consultant and Meditation Facilitator to create powerful, inspiring thought provoking seminars.

In her spare time she loves all things artistic, poetry, writing, songwriting painting, photography, singing and dancing. In all artistic pursuits she celebrates the idea that we are all 'Spiritual Beings having a human experience.' Whether travelling the world, sitting in the tropical sunlight of northern Queensland, Bali or in the wilds of Tasmania, her current home state, she continues to draw upon her personal experiences to help others look deeper into themselves.

www.ingramcontent.com/pod-product-compliance
Lightning Source LLC
Chambersburg PA
CBHW040551010526
44110CB00054B/2621